A TRUE BOOK™

Why It Matters

The
U.S. Congress

Melissa McDaniel

Children's Press®
An Imprint of Scholastic Inc.

Content Consultant
Saikrishna Bangalore Prakash
James Monroe Distinguished Professor of Law
Paul G. Mahoney Research Professor of Law
Miller Center Senior Fellow
University of Virginia
Charlottesville, Virginia

Teacher Adviser
Rachel Hsieh

Library of Congress Cataloging-in-Publication Data
Names: McDaniel, Melissa, 1964– author.
Title: The U.S. Congress : why it matters to you / Melissa McDaniel.
Description: New York : Children's Press, an imprint of Scholastic, 2020. | Series: A true book | Includes
    bibliographical references and index.
Identifiers: LCCN 2019004800 | ISBN 9780531231821 (library binding) | ISBN 9780531239940 (pbk.)
Subjects: LCSH: United States. Congress—Juvenile literature. | United States—Politics and government—
    Juvenile literature.
Classification: LCC JK1025 .M33 2020 | DDC 328.73—dc23
LC record available at https://lccn.loc.gov/2019004800

All rights reserved. Published in 2020 by Children's Press, an imprint of Scholastic Inc.
Printed in North Mankato, MN, USA 113

SCHOLASTIC, CHILDREN'S PRESS, A TRUE BOOK™, and associated logos are trademarks and/or
registered trademarks of Scholastic Inc.

Scholastic Inc., 557 Broadway, New York, NY 10012

1 2 3 4 5 6 7 8 9 10 R 29 28 27 26 25 24 23 22 21 20

Front cover: U.S. Capitol
**Back cover: Members of the Senate and
House of Representatives in a joint session**

Find the Truth!

Everything you are about to read is true *except* for one of the sentences on this page.

Which one is **TRUE**?

T or F More than half the members of Congress are women.

T or F Congress has the power to remove the president from office.

Find the answers in this book.

Contents

New citizens

Senator Hiram
Revels

Think About It!

Whoosh! A geyser at Yellowstone National Park shoots superheated water high into the sky. Every year, millions of people visit the park to see spectacular sights like this. Anyone can, including you! What does this have to do with Congress? And what does Congress have to do with you?

Intrigued?
Want to know more? Turn the page!

George Washington (in black) led the convention where the U.S. Constitution was written.

Did you guess that Congress created Yellowstone National Park? If so, you were right! Every year, Congress makes decisions that affect your family. These decisions include the 1872 law protecting Yellowstone and opening the land to visitors like you.

After the United States won its independence from Great Britain in 1783, American leaders faced difficult questions. Who should have power? Who should make laws? State representatives met in 1787 and settled these questions by writing a **constitution**.

The Constitution created a **republic** in which citizens vote for representatives to make government decisions. Power is spread among three branches, or parts. The executive branch enforces laws. The president leads it. The **federal** courts of the judicial branch interpret laws and strike them down if they don't follow the Constitution. But first, the legislative branch—Congress—writes the laws. These decisions touch the lives of everyone in the nation, including yours.

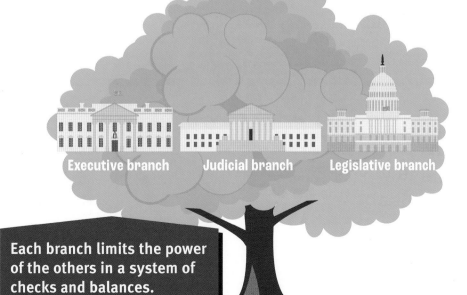

Executive branch   Judicial branch   Legislative branch

Each branch limits the power of the others in a system of checks and balances.

Senator Tammy Duckworth joins a parade in Oak Park, Illinois.

Tammy Duckworth of Illinois is the first woman with a disability to serve in Congress.

CHAPTER

1

The Way to Washington, D.C.

Do you have what it takes to be a member of Congress? Are you good at working with other people? Are you ready to become an expert on many subjects? Do you want to work hard for the people who live in your area? Do you like being on TV? Can you brush off criticism? If so, then you might be a great congressperson.

The House and Senate sometimes meet together in what is called a joint session of Congress.

The Structure of Congress

The U.S. Congress is made up of two parts: the Senate and the House of Representatives. The Senate has 100 members. Two senators come from each state.

The House of Representatives has 435 members. The number of representatives each state has varies. Each state has at least one representative. The more people who live in a state, the more representatives it has. Each member of the House represents a district that is home to an average of about 750,000 people.

Who Can Serve in Congress?

To become members of Congress, people must be U.S. citizens. Congresspeople must also live in the state that elected them. Representatives have to be at least 25 years old when they take office. Senators have to be at least 30.

A big difference between representatives and senators is that representatives serve two-year terms. Senators are elected for six years.

Representative Liz Cheney (in red) takes her oath of office in 2017.

Vote for Me!

A candidate meets voters.

Being elected to Congress takes time and money. **Candidates** need to travel to all parts of their district to meet voters. They speak in schools, in restaurants, and on street corners to discuss issues. They also pay for ads on television, radio, and in print.

In the United States, most candidates belong to either the Democratic or Republican Party. Each party holds a primary election to determine its candidate. The winners then compete in the general election to see who goes to Washington, D.C.

VOTE WISNOSKY

Signs, television commercials, and other advertisements cost money. Why do you think candidates need them? How do they help a campaign?

"If I could afford a plane, I'd hire a plane."

Living in Washington, D.C.

Congratulations! You've been elected to Congress! Now what? You can't just move to Washington, D.C., because you'd like to stay connected to your home district. So what do you do?

Some congresspeople rent a house in Washington, D.C., but it's expensive paying for two homes. Some lawmakers share a house. Others just sleep in their offices. They shower in the gym in the basement of the Capitol. Regardless of where they sleep, most congresspeople head home every weekend.

In 2007, Democrat Nancy Pelosi became the first female speaker of the house.

Nancy Pelosi poses with the children and grandchildren of congresspeople upon becoming speaker of the house.

On the Job

Congress's leaders are among the most powerful people in Washington, D.C. The party with the most seats in each house chooses who heads that house. Those leaders then control what **bills**, or proposed laws, are considered. The Senate's top legislative official is called the senate majority leader. The speaker of the house runs the House of Representatives. If the president and vice president both died or were forced to leave office, the speaker would become president.

The Capitol

The chambers where senators and representatives vote are located in the Capitol. The Capitol was completed in 1826. The British burned an earlier version to the ground during the War of 1812, but it was rebuilt and expanded in the years after. Today the Capitol, topped with its grand dome, is one of the most famous buildings in Washington, D.C. Tunnels connect the Capitol to nearby congressional office buildings. These buildings contain the offices of congresspeople.

On average, congresspeople introduce more than 6,000 bills each year. Only 3 to 4 percent become law.

The U.S. Congress is sometimes referred to as Capitol Hill, after the neighborhood where the Capitol is located.

Becoming an Expert

Each congressperson is part of several committees. The committees specialize in different subjects, such as the environment or the budget, which is how money is spent. The congresspeople who sit on each committee become experts in that field.

Each bill that is introduced in Congress is first sent to the committee related to its subject. The committee can discuss the bill and make changes to it.

As bills are discussed, sections get crossed out and added.

Passing Bills and Budgets

Often, Democrats and Republicans have different views on issues. Sometimes they can compromise, or find a middle ground, on a bill or budget.

When a committee approves a bill, it is sent to the full House or Senate. Members are given time to **debate** the bill before voting on it. A bill must pass in both the House and the Senate before it is sent to the president to be signed into law.

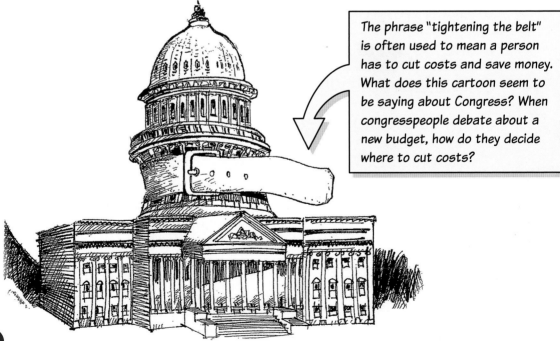

The phrase "tightening the belt" is often used to mean a person has to cut costs and save money. What does this cartoon seem to be saying about Congress? When congresspeople debate about a new budget, how do they decide where to cut costs?

The Power to Say No

Who has more power, Congress or the president? Ideally, their power is balanced. This is thanks to the government's system of checks and balances.

Before a bill becomes law, the president typically must sign it. But sometimes the president vetoes, or rejects, a bill instead of signing it. That does not always mean the bill is dead, however. If two-thirds of both the House and Senate vote to override the veto, the bill becomes law.

President Donald Trump vetoes a bill in 2019.

PUBLIC SCHOOL

"I was nominated to be class president but I dread the confirmation hearings. I hope they don't bring up my questionable behavior in preschool."

At confirmation hearings, senators can ask about a nominee's past. What is the cartoon suggesting about such questions?

a.bacall

Beyond Bills

Congress does more than pass bills. The Constitution grants Congress the power to declare war. For example, in 1941, Japanese bombers attacked Pearl Harbor, Hawaii. Congress then passed a declaration of war on Japan. This brought the United States into World War II (1939–1945).

The Senate also confirms, or approves, Supreme Court justices and other important officials **nominated** by the president. Senators hold hearings to question nominees and people who know the nominees.

Investigations

Congress has the power to conduct investigations. Sometimes Congress investigates possible wrongdoing. Other times it looks into problems in the government or the country.

Congress can even investigate the president. The House can impeach, or bring charges against, a president for committing treason or high crimes. Presidents Andrew Johnson and Bill Clinton were impeached, but neither was found guilty.

Senators Cory Booker (left) and Kamala Harris (right) take part in a congressional investigation.

Each year, industries spend more than $3 billion lobbying in Washington, D.C.

K
1700

ST
NW

The lobbying industry is sometimes known as K Street because so many lobbying firms are located on this street in Washington, D.C.

The People Speak

Congress impacts your life in many ways. Congressional actions affect the tests you take at school, how clean your drinking water is, and the conditions of the roads in your town. The work of the government touches all kinds of people, businesses, and organizations. Who has the power to influence Congress? Who do congresspeople listen to as they make their decisions?

Research

Congresspeople gather information in many ways. Committees can hold hearings on issues. Experts and people affected by an issue speak at the hearings. For example, a committee might ask scientists to come speak about the effect of oil drilling on endangered wildlife.

People who work for congresspeople and committees can also help them collect information.

Hundreds of people testify before Congress each year. In 2018, Facebook's Mark Zuckerberg spent two days answering hundreds of questions during a congressional hearing.

In this cartoon, Congress performs as a puppet for Wall Street, where a lot of the country's financial business occurs. What does this suggest about the power of business over Congress?

Lobbyists

Lobbyists also affect the votes of congresspeople. These are people who are hired to influence Congress. Many lobbyists work for individual companies. Some are hired by organizations that work on behalf of entire industries, such as drug manufacturers. And some work for groups concerned with specific issues, such as the environment. Most of the money spent on lobbying comes from businesses and corporations.

A congressperson speaks at a town hall meeting in Massachusetts.

Making Your Voice Heard

Congresspeople also want to hear from people who live in their district. Some senators and representatives hold town hall meetings to find out what people think. Calling your congressperson is another very good way to let them know your views. This is especially true when there is an important vote coming up. Congressional offices keep a tally of whether callers are for or against an issue.

Loud and Clear

Sometimes citizens gather in large demonstrations to try and make their voices heard. In 2018, a group of young people from Parkland, Florida, became activists. They started working to change gun laws after a shooting at their high school. They met with congresspeople to talk about the issue. But they also led large demonstrations. Large protests can make it loud and clear to Congress that many people believe things need to change.

Demonstrations take advantage of the freedom of speech, which is guaranteed in the Bill of Rights.

In 1789, when the first Congress was elected, only 6 percent of the population could vote.

Women count ballots at a polling place in Massachusetts in the 1950s.

Creating Our System

The **delegates** who formed the U.S. government had to agree on one system. But some states were small. Others were large. In some states, enslaved African Americans were a big part of the population but were not given the power to vote at the time. The delegates created a two-house legislature. The Senate gave each state equal representation. House representation was based on population. Only three of every five enslaved people were accounted for in each state.

Expanding Democracy

Democracy is important in our republic. Americans vote freely on their leaders. When Congress was created, though, the vote was usually limited to white men who owned property. This has changed gradually. After the Civil War (1861–1865), Congress granted African American men the right to vote. Yet many states still found ways to keep them from voting. It was not until the 1960s that new laws would try to better protect voting and other rights.

Timeline of Congressional Milestones

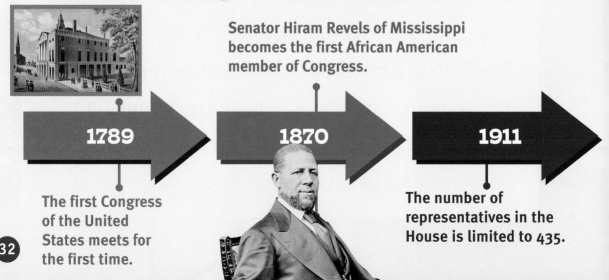

Senator Hiram Revels of Mississippi becomes the first African American member of Congress.

1789

1870

1911

The first Congress of the United States meets for the first time.

The number of representatives in the House is limited to 435.

Other groups have also been kept out of the voting booth. Women across the nation were first given the vote in 1920. Native Americans were granted citizenship in 1924. It took four more decades for them to be granted voting rights in all 50 states.

The vote has also evolved in another way. Under the Constitution, state legislators, not the people, chose U.S. senators. In 1913, the 17th **Amendment** changed this. Now senators, like representatives, are elected directly by popular vote.

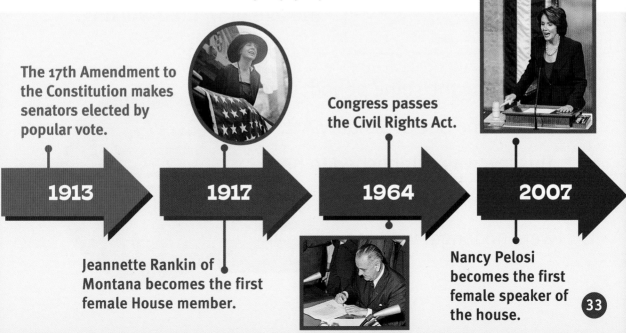

The 17th Amendment to the Constitution makes senators elected by popular vote.

Congress passes the Civil Rights Act.

1913

1917

1964

2007

Jeannette Rankin of Montana becomes the first female House member.

Nancy Pelosi becomes the first female speaker of the house.

Making History

Throughout U.S. history, Congress has passed laws that help you and your family. In the early 20th century, many children were forced to work in dangerous mines and factories. The Fair Labor Standards Act of 1938 barred children under the age of 14 from working, except on farms.

During the same period, Congress passed the Social Security Act. This law was established to help support the elderly who were no longer working.

Children working in a mine

Changing Times

Sometimes Congress builds on past actions. In the 1960s, Congress established Medicare. This system provides health care to people who retire, or stop working. Then in 1997, Congress began a program providing poor children with health care.

Other times, Congress reverses course. In 1882, a law banned Chinese people from immigrating to the United States. This law was **repealed** in 1943. Then the Immigration Act of 1965 made the system fairer to people from around the world.

Children wave flags after becoming U.S. citizens.

Two Senators per State?

Each state has two senators regardless of its population. Some states, however, have big cities that are densely populated. Other states have a lot of land devoted to farming or other use, and few people live there. California, for example, has 80 times the population of Wyoming, yet each has two senators. Some people argue this makes things unfair.

What do you think?

Rural areas have very small populations. In cities, people are much more densely packed.

Should states continue to have two senators each?

YES	NO
✔ The delegates who helped write the Constitution decided this was the best course.	✔ Some delegates were against representing each state equally, rather than each person equally. They argued it was unfair to the people.
✔ Each state has the same amount of power in the Senate.	✔ The way people live has changed. Far fewer people live in rural areas today, compared to the early United States.
✔ Rural states, with low populations, have the same power as states with large populations, so Congress cannot ignore the interests of rural states.	✔ Individuals in rural areas have more people representing them in Congress than those in urban areas. This gives rural people more power in Congress.
✔ The House of Representatives is divided according to population. This helps balance Congress.	✔ The percentage of Americans living in urban centers will only grow. By 2040, 70 percent of Americans will live in 15 states. This means that just 30 senators will represent 70 percent of the population. The remaining 30 percent of people will have 70 senators.

In 2019, Congress had the largest number of female members in U.S. history.

Congresswomen serving in the House of Representatives pose for a photo.

CHAPTER 5

The Changing Face of Congress

Does Congress look like you? Do members have the same kind of wealth or lifestyle you do? Does it matter?

Over the years, Congress has slowly begun to look more like our nation. For example, women make up slightly more than half of the population. But it was not until 1917 that Jeannette Rankin became the first female member of Congress. By 2019, nearly a quarter of congresspeople were women.

A Mirror of the Nation

In recent years, more young people have run for Congress—and won. They also come from more diverse backgrounds. In 2018, Native American women and Muslim women were elected to Congress for the first time. The numbers of Latinos, African Americans, and Asians in Congress are also growing. But there is still work to be done. Roughly 40 percent of the people in the country belong to a minority group. But only a quarter of congresspeople are minorities.

Sharice Davids of Kansas was one of the first Native American women elected to Congress.

Candidates should fight for issues they care about. But what about the public? In this cartoon, a candidate is speaking before members of the public. What does it say about the importance of public opinion? How might that affect a candidate's actions?

What Would You Do?

Would you like to be a member of Congress? Think about the issues that are most important to you and your community. Do you want to pass laws that help maintain a healthy environment for future generations? Do you want to make sure that you pay low taxes? Perhaps you want to make sure that all people have access to health care. Whatever issues you care about, Congress is a place where you can make a difference. Congress matters!

Fighting for Equality

Kids cannot vote, but they can still tell Congress how they feel about important issues.

Some young people have made their voices heard and have made a difference.

In 1963 in Alabama, thousands of young people took part in the Birmingham Children's Crusade. They were peacefully protesting segregation, or separation according to race, and other unfair treatment they had all experienced.

The police responded violently. They beat the

Police lead young children to jail for protesting in Alabama in 1963.

young protesters with batons and sprayed them with fire hoses. These images were shown on TV, shocking the nation and the world.

The brave actions of the young people raised awareness about discrimination, or unfair treatment, in the United States. These and other protests showed congresspeople that laws needed to change. Congress passed the Civil Rights Act of 1964, which outlaws discrimination based on race, sex, religion, or national origin.

Young activists still have work to do. Asean Johnson went all the way to Washington, D.C. in 2013 to speak out about school closings in his home of Chicago, Illinois. He was 12 years old at the time. Others, such as Katie Eder, focus on encouraging kids and teens to make their own voices heard.

Get Involved!

You're too young to vote for your representatives, but there are a lot of things you can do to be an active citizen:

Attend events with your family where you can talk to your representative about issues.

Read reliable news sources to stay up-to-date on what is happening in the world.

Write to the people who represent your state in Congress about issues that are important to you. You can find their official email and mailing addresses online.

Encourage your family members to register and vote.

Did you find the truth?

 More than half the members of Congress are women.

Congress has the power to remove the president from office.

Resources

The book you just read is a first introduction to the U.S. Congress, and to the history and government of our country. There is always more to learn and discover. In addition to this title, we encourage you to seek out complementary resources.

Other books in this series:

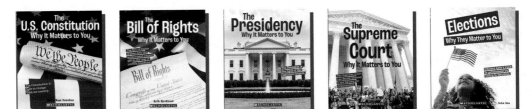

You can also look at:

Clark-Robinson, Monica. *Let the Children March*. New York: Houghton, Mifflin, Harcourt, 2018.

Cooper, Ilene. *A Woman in the House (and Senate): How Women Came to the United States Congress, Broke Down Barriers, and Changed the Country*. New York: Abrams Books for Young Readers, 2014.

Rawson, Katherine. *U.S. Capitol*. Minneapolis: Bullfrog Books, 2018.

Small, Cathleen. *How Does Congress Work?* Farmington Hills, MI: Lucent Books, 2018.

Glossary

amendment (uh-MEND-muhnt) a change that is made to a law or legal document, especially the Constitution

bills (BILZ) written plans for a new law, to be debated and passed by a body of legislators

candidates (KAN-duh-dates) people who are applying for a job or running in an election

constitution (kahn-stih-TOO-shuhn) the basic laws of a country that state the rights of the people and the powers of the government

debate (dih-BATE) to discuss or think about something from different points of view

delegates (DEHL-uh-gits) people who represent others at a meeting or in a legislature

democracy (di-MAH-kruh-see) a form of government in which the people choose their leaders in elections

federal (FED-ur-uhl) national; describing a system of government in which states are united under a central authority

nominated (NAH-muh-nay-tid) suggested as a good person for an important job or to receive an honor

repealed (rih-PEELD) canceled or done away with officially

republic (rih-PUB-lik) a form of government in which the people elect representatives who manage the government

Index

Page numbers in **bold** indicate illustrations.

About the Author

Melissa McDaniel is the author of more than 30 books for young people. She was born in Portland, Oregon, and now lives in New York City, where she works as a writer and editor.